Why Do Germans Say That?

Copyright © 2025 Max Skalla and Werner Skalla. All rights reserved.
Published by Skapago Publishing, Von-Müller-Str. 12, 93437 Furth im Wald,
Germany. Contact to the publisher: info@skapago.eu, +49 9975 206330

Edited by Pilla Leitner & Werner Skalla
1st edition published in March 2025

No part of this publication may be reproduced, stored in a retrieval system, or transmitted in any form or by any means, electronic, mechanical, photocopying, recording, scanning, or otherwise, except as permitted by law, without the prior written permission of the Publisher. Requests to the Publisher for permission can be addressed to info@skapago.eu.

Links published in this book are accessible at the time of publication. The publisher cannot guarantee accessibility in the future.

ISBN Softcover: 978-3-945174-34-0
ISBN Hardcover: 978-3-945174-35-7
ISBN eBook: 978-3-945174-36-4

Free bonus materials to this book:
https://www.skapago.eu/jensjakob/idioms-bonus/

Learn languages with Skapago
German: Jens und Jakob, ISBN 978-3-945174-06-7
Swedish: Alfred the Ghost, ISBN 978-3-945174-10-4
Norwegian: The Mystery of Nils, ISBN 978-3-945174-30-2
Chinese: Oh, Jerry!, ISBN 978-3-945174-16-6

Other languages at www.skapago.eu

Why do Germans say that? 2
German expressions in comic strips

Text & illustrations
Max. Skalla

9 Edibles:
10 Eine Extrawurst bekommen
12 Mit jemandem ist nicht gut Kirschen essen
14 Saure-Gurken-Zeit
16 Jemandem die Suppe versalzen
18 Wie Kraut und Rüben
20 Jemanden durch den Kakao ziehen
22 Abwarten und Tee trinken
24 Die Suppe auslöffeln müssen
26 Da haben wir den Salat
28 Nicht aus Zucker sein
30 Es geht um die Wurst
32 Reinen Wein einschenken

35 People:
36 Der Koch ist verliebt
38 Unter den Blinden ist der Einäugige König
40 Da scheiden sich die Geister
42 Milchmädchenrechnung
44 Was Hänschen nicht lernt, lernt Hans nimmermehr
46 Der dümmste Bauer hat die dicksten Kartoffeln
48 Pech im Spiel, Glück in der Liebe

51 Animals:
52 Jemandem ist eine Laus über die Leber gelaufen
54 Das ist eine Ente
56 Ein Pechvogel sein
58 Ein Fischkopf sein
60 Einen Pferdefuß haben
62 Den Bock zum Gärtner machen
64 Mit jemandem Pferde stehlen können
66 Sich mit fremden Federn schmücken

69 Places:
70 Leben wie Gott in Frankreich
72 Gang nach Canossa
74 Einmal hü und einmal hott sagen
76 Schwedische Gardinen
78 Hinter dem Mond leben
80 Was für ein Tohuwabohu

83 Clothes and body:
84 Das letzte Hemd hat keine Taschen
86 Alte Zöpfe abschneiden
88 Hals- und Beinbruch!
90 Jacke wie Hose
92 Das passt wie die Faust aufs Auge
94 Haare auf den Zähnen haben
96 Das Handtuch werfen

99 Objects:
100 Im Eimer sein
102 Auf dem Holzweg sein
104 Jemanden über den grünen Klee loben
106 In die Röhre gucken
108 Auf dem Schlauch stehen
110 Es ist höchste Eisenbahn
112 Buch mit sieben Siegeln
114 Etwas auf dem Schirm haben
116 Durch den Wind sein
118 In ein Loch fallen

120 Skapago

www.skapago.com
If you took the time to tilt and read then drop by our website.
– We don't bite!

info@skapago.eu
Send us a message if you have any questions, or just to simply say hello.

Hello again,

I'm excited to share my second book with you, where I recount my hilarious journey navigating the twists and turns of the German language and culture during a global pandemic, when the first book was born.

Through a series of trial-and-error moments, I discovered the beauty of the German language, but soon found myself face-to-face with the infamous linguistic monster we call "idioms" that left me scratching my head: Why do Germans say that? I was determined to uncover the secrets behind these enigmatic expressions.

As I delved deeper into the world of German idioms, I realized that even native speakers might be mystified by their origins and meanings. I decided to tap into my creative side and use funny child-like drawings to bring these idioms to life. By combining comic-style strips with relatable characters, I aimed to make learning German idioms an enjoyable and engaging experience, while giving a glimpse into the history and context behind their meanings, helping you understand the nuances of the culture.

May you have as much fun with it as I did creating it.

Enjoy.

1 Eine Extrawurst bekommen
2 Mit jemandem ist nicht gut Kirschen essen
3 Saure-Gurken-Zeit
4 Jemandem die Suppe versalzen
5 Wie Kraut und Rüben
6 Jemanden durch den Kakao ziehen
7 Abwarten und Tee trinken
8 Die Suppe auslöffeln müssen
9 Da haben wir den Salat
10 Nicht aus Zucker sein
11 Es geht um die Wurst
12 Reinen Wein einschenken

– … No! … No! … Disgusting!
– Banana with Banana filled with Banana.
– He wants to get an extra sausage.

What? Literally: To receive an extra / special sausage.
Means: Getting special treatment.

How? This idiom is all about receiving something special, and often for free! It's a lovely expression that captures the surprise and delight of getting a little something extra to brighten up your day. Like a lunch menu offer with a free dessert included. If you're unlucky you'd hear "In this company nobody receives an extra sausage": Everyone is equal and nobody will receive any extra treatment.

Why? There are some sources dating back to the Middle Ages that say that sausages were a special delicacy for the poor, and vendors would sometimes add an extra *Wurst* to bring a smile to their day. For Germans, nothing brings more joy than a free sausage – a tofu sausage in case you're vegan.

– Did I forget to feed the cat?
– Oh dear, that's going to cause trouble.
It is not good to eat cherries with cats.

Mit jemandem ist nicht gut Kirschen essen

What? Literally: It's not good to eat cherries with someone.
Means: A difficult person to get along with.

How? We've all encountered that one person – a difficult and stubborn friend, colleague, or boss who's inflexible and hard to please. Avoid the stress and negativity that comes with them. It's best to keep a safe distance and enjoy your peace, perhaps by indulging in cherries which you don't waste on them.

Why? Another idiom dating back to the Middle Ages, when people used to say it is not advisable to eat cherries with nobility because they'll spit the seeds in your face … ew.

Another backstory might be an incident from the 13th century, when the Bishop of Meissen reconciled with his rival, the Margrave of Meissen, by giving him a peace offering: poisoned cherries! He died a sweet death shortly after. It should be called "It's poisonous to eat cherries with him."

– Ice-cream.
– Winter is a pickle time for ice-cream.

Saure-Gurken-Zeit

What? Literally: Pickle time.
Means: low season.

How? To describe a low season for a certain activity. January is a low season for productivity, as everyone was exhausted from buying gifts and running around buying ingredients to bake Christmas *Plätzchen* and partying for New Year's. Now they're ready to relax and make pickles, while pretending that learning German is their New Year's resolution.

Why? It comes from a very unexpected term derived from Yiddish in Berlin, referring to the period of suffering and inflation called Zores and Jokreszeit. The term got reinterpreted and added to the colloquial etymology as *Gurkenzeit* mostly due to the close similarity in its pronunciation.

– National Soup Competition.
– The day before.
– I oversalted their soup.

Jemandem die Suppe versalzen

What? Literally: To oversalt someone's soup.
Means: To spoil someone's plans.

How? When plans go astray, it can be due to either unintentional or intentional circumstances. Unexpected events like bad weather during an event – "I'm excited for the picnic tomorrow, but the rain might salt the soup" – or an intentional act of sabotage meant to cause inconvenience, like bringing only one controller to a game night with friends as revenge for them forgetting your birthday. I mean why would you do such an atrocious act?

Why? Unfortunately, there are no records of its origin, although the expression has been used for hundreds of years. I assume that oversalting someone's food ruins the taste, even though I personally prefer my food salty. In that case, it won't spoil my plans.

– Already packed?
– The things are lying in the suitcase like cabbage and turnips.

Wie Kraut und Rüben

What? Literally: Like cabbage and turnips.
Means: Jumbled mess.

How? When you see something messy and confusing, like a complicated train network on a map, where you have no idea where the line begins and ends, or a friend's apartment after celebrating New Year's and making a mess. Even worse when you see a German grammar table.

Why? It dates back to the 17th century, and it may have originated from the historical practice of farms planting cabbage and turnips mixed together, which resulted in a messy appearance compared to vegetables that were planted neatly separately.

– Your cake smells funny …
– Your candle too … you too … you pig
– He's really pulling him through cocoa.

Jemanden durch den Kakao ziehen

What? Literally: To pull someone through cocoa.
Means: To criticize and make fun of someone.

How? To mock and joke around. It can be a lighthearted situation, like watching a terrible movie and wondering if the director is intentionally poking fun at the audience, trying to pull them through the "chocolate" of absurdity. Or, it can be a more hurtful experience, like when a friend teases you and makes jokes at your expense, laughing at your German accent when you try to pronounce "Ü", which ironically looks like a smiley.

Why? It may date back to the 20th century and has connotations with another word, "Kacke", which means "poopy", due to the similar pronunciation between "Kakao" and "Kacke". I prefer the "chocolate" version, which I wouldn't mind being literally pulled through.

– Delay approx. 29 hours.
– Let's wait and drink tea.

What? Literally: To wait and drink tea.
Means: Wait and see.

How? Your friend has ordered something online and is anxiously waiting for his package to arrive. He's been jumping around the room, checking his watch and refreshing his email for any new notifications. You suggest he relax and be patient, and brew a cup of tea to calm him down. It can also describe a non-definite result. When you don't know when your favorite artist will publish their new *Why Do Germans Say That* book, you have no choice but to relax and wait.

Why? One of the earliest written records of the saying dates back to the 19th century, when herbalist Philipp Heinrich Schäfer recommended that doctors give their patients herbal tea and wait for its healing properties to take effect. Tea was introduced to Germany in the 17th century and was associated with relaxation and taking time off.

– She has to spoon out the soup.

Die Suppe auslöffeln müssen

What? Literally: To scoop out the soup.
Means: To face the consequences.

How? This saying derives from the idea that everyone must bear the consequences of their own actions. Your friend calls you up asking for help with his homework, saying he completely overslept and partied all weekend long. You think he should take responsibility for his actions and tell him, "You should eat your own soup."

Why? It may date back to a text from Terentius Afer, a Roman poet and comedy writer, who lived before Christ. He wrote "Tute hoc intristi, tibi omne est exedendum", which translates literally to "You stirred it; you have to spoon it out".

– Your brother will cook today? Really?
– Don't worry …
– Here we have the salad.

Da haben wir den Salat

What? Literally: There we have the salad.
Means: Something unpleasant happens.

How? When something goes wrong and the result of the mess becomes apparent. You're not sure if the sofa you ordered online will fit through the door, and when it arrives, you realize it doesn't. You stand there near the door, staring at the awkwardly-shaped piece of furniture, and think to yourself, "Now we have the salad!"

Why? Since the 19th century, the word "salad" has been used to describe chaos, as salads are often messy. Interestingly, Germans also use the term "Kabelsalat" (cable salad) to describe a tangled mess of cables.

– Oh, we can't go out. It's raining.
– Oh, come on, you're not made of sugar.

What? Literally: Not made of sugar.
Means: To handle the rain.

How? The most common meaning is to be able to withstand the rain. It happened to me and my friends when we visited Amsterdam and they weren't used to the rain. They looked out of the apartment window and said, "Oh, we can't go out for dinner, it's raining!" As if a little rain would stop us, we're not made of sugar! Another meaning, however, is more abstract. When you can overcome challenges because you're tough, and tougher than sugar, you can handle them. For example, I'll memorize these idioms because I'm smart enough.

Why? This one is self-explanatory, as sugar dissolves in liquid. Its origin is unknown, but I wonder why sugar was chosen, rather than salt. Even though I think sugar is sweet, I don't mind being fragile, and sweet as sugar.

– Rock, paper, scissors! The winner eats the last sausage.
– Last round ... Now it's all about the sausage!

Es geht um die Wurst

What? Literally: It's about the sausage.
Means: A critical moment.

How? I love these idioms, especially the German obsession for sausages. They're used to describe any critical moment when things are getting serious. For example, imagine a Eurovision contest and this is the last performance before the winner is chosen. Or a football match and this is the final round. In any case, nothing is more motivating than the promise of a sausage.

Why? The idiom is recorded as early as the 19th century. It may be related to *Wurstschnappen*, a traditional contest where participants attempt to catch sausages suspended on a string with their mouths. It is quite a funny contest. You should look it up.

– Pour us pure wine, are we bankrupt or not?

Reinen Wein einschenken

What? Literally: To pour out pure wine.
Means: To tell the bitter truth.

How? If you have something unpleasant you need to share. For instance, you have a crush on someone and your boyfriend or girlfriend doesn't know and you ought to tell them the bitter truth. You "pour them some pure wine". Or you find out that your colleague is getting fired and you feel obliged to let them know.

Why? A trick from the Middle Ages, when bar keepers would water down wine or mix it with vinegar in order to make it last longer and increase their profits. Those who served their customers genuine, undiluted pure wine were considered to be honest and trustworthy. Therefore, to tell someone the whole truth, frankly, is like pouring pure wine.

1 Der Koch ist verliebt
2 Unter den Blinden ist der Einäugige König
3 Da scheiden sich die Geister
4 Milchmädchenrechnung
5 Was Hänschen nicht lernt, lernt Hans nimmermehr
6 Der dümmste Bauer hat die dicksten Kartoffeln
7 Pech im Spiel, Glück in der Liebe

– Oh, good luck next time. Let me try the soup.
– Too salty.
– The chef is in love.

Der Koch ist verliebt

What? Literally: The chef is in love.
Means: The food is too salty.

How? This idiom is quite straightforward: when the food is too salty, it's said that the chef is in love with you. It's a humorous excuse to overindulge in salty food while ignoring high blood pressure risks and claiming it's a romantic gesture. Wouldn't that imply that bland food is reserved for enemies?

Why? Salt has been a highly valued and expensive material for centuries, dating back to ancient Greece, where it was believed to have aphrodisiac properties and that a lack of it could compromise male potency. As a result, lovers would often oversalt their food when they could afford it. Even as far back as the 16th century, the phrase "salting your partner" became a widespread expression. Interestingly, from our current perspective, we would view sugar as a more obvious symbol of sweet love.

– READY, SET, GO!
– That was easy! Among the blind, the one-eyed man is king.

Unter den Blinden ist der Einäugige König

What? Literally: Among the blind, the one-eyed man is king.
Means: Among the unqualified, the mediocre is great.

How? When your friend gets promoted, you might think to yourself, "Damn, he's not very good at his job." You might reason that the competition is low, and he's the best of the worst. This twisted perspective can bring a sense of relief, as it suggests that as long as those around you are worse than you, you'll be considered the best. It's a peculiar, negative, and cynical way to look at it, but it can be a comforting thought. It reminds me of my poor eyesight, and buying transparent glasses frames was a bad idea. I have trouble finding them every time I misplace them. Poor me.

Why? This proverb is heard in many different cultures across Europe. For example, the Italians and the French share a similar expression, although it is formulated slightly differently. The phrase may have originated from a Bible verse in Matthew 15:14, which states: "If a blind man leads a blind man, both will fall into a pit." It is often used as a comforting way to say that you don't have to be the best, but rather only better than the competition.

– And now for the pandemic round. Masks or no masks.
– Mr. Scientist. Ms. Scientist.
– Whether masks or not, spirits are divided.

Da scheiden sich die Geister

What? Literally: That's where the spirits separate.
Means: Opinions differ.

How? When there are two conflicting opinions on a subject, it's often a matter of personal taste or perspective. For example, whether Germany should impose speed limits on the Autobahn or not is a controversial issue, where spirits separate. Similarly, whether this book you are currently reading is great or amazing is a subjective choice, as opinions on this topic differ drastically.

Why? The word "Geist" has a similar meaning to "ghost" or "spooky creatures," but in this expression, it refers to the human spirit and mind. Since we are all individuals with separate souls, we possess different opinions and emotions on any topic. In German, the term "Geisteswissenschaften" refers to the science of the mind or humanities, encompassing fields such as philosophy, history, music, linguistics, and religion, among others. Similarly, the subjective nature of these topics is mirrored in our opinions and desires.

– Why is there poverty?
– They should simply print more money.
– Such a Milkmaid's calculation!

Milchmädchenrechnung

What? Literally: Milkmaid's calculation.
Means: A naive opinion.

How? This refers to when someone calculates something incorrectly or reaches a naive conclusion without considering important details. For example, if a political party suggests that we simply drop all ticket fees for public transport without planning or thinking about who or what will cover the costs of such a decision, that's a "Milkmaid's calculation", implying that it's a simplistic, naive and unrealistic idea.

Why? The expression is believed to have originated from a fable by the German poet Johann Wilhelm Ludwig Gleim, which was inspired by a French poet Jean de La Fontaine's work in the 17th century. The fable is titled "Das Milchmädchen und der Milchtopf" (The Milkmaid and the Milk Pot). The story revolves around a milkmaid who calculates that the money she earns from selling milk will buy a chicken, which will then produce eggs to purchase a pig, and ultimately a cow. However, her plans are foiled when she accidentally spills the milk, making her calculations irrelevant.

- I will never reach her level. She started riding at a young age.
- Indeed! What little Hans doesn't learn, Hans will never learn.

Was Hänschen nicht lernt, lernt Hans nimmermehr

What? Literally: What Little Hans doesn't learn, Hans will never learn.
Means: You learn better in youth than in old age.

How? This is the classic excuse to avoid learning something new. When adults say that you can't learn German unless you start from a young age, or that you can't learn to ride a bike unless you start as a child, that's when the expression comes into play. It's often used when age is cited as the reason for not being able to understand a particular topic, or when someone claims it's too late to learn a hobby, such as playing the piano. However, ironically, there is no legal age limit in Germany for studying.

Why? Hans is a commonly used male first name to refer to a person in general, similar to "Joe" in English. The idea that age matters for learning has its roots in ancient times, but this idiom is often attributed to Martin Luther, who used it to caution his students to learn as much as they could now, before it is too late. Unfortunately, this phrase is often repeated in schools, and it has a somewhat pessimistic tone. At least to me, I find it a bit discouraging. For it ain't late until you're dead.

– Is your first potato farm going well?
– Well, the dumbest farmer has the biggest potatoes.

Der dümmste Bauer hat die dicksten Kartoffeln

What? Literally: The dumbest farmer has the biggest potatoes.
Means: Achieving success without much effort.

How? It is generally used to describe people who achieve something without deserving it or even working hard for it. We all know a person who succeeds with minimal effort: The singer who belts out two notes and becomes the richest musician on the planet, or the artist who strokes a brush on a canvas and earns millions. Success often entails a sense of naivety and courage. While one farmer overthinks and plans his crops too much, the other farmer is already planting and ends up with the biggest potatoes.

Why? Farming is often unfairly associated with a lack of intelligence. There's a belief that cultivating potatoes doesn't require exceptional intellectual abilities, and success often stems from taking action rather than overthinking. It seems like jealousy to me, as it's hard for many people to comprehend how someone can achieve success without being less intelligent or undeserving. I'd rather say someone is *bauernschlau*, being as clever as a farmer.

– Unlucky in games, lucky in love.

Pech im Spiel, Glück in der Liebe

What? Literally: Unlucky in games, lucky in love.
Means: You can't be lucky in everything.

How? When someone's really struggling with a particular skill, but they're surrounded by loved ones, you can offer them some comfort by saying, "Unlucky in games, lucky in love." It's similar to the English proverb, "unlucky at cards, lucky in love." This phrase is a great way to lift someone's spirits when they're feeling down about their performance. For example, imagine you're bowling with a friend who's getting knocked down every time. You could try cheering them up with this German expression. And as for me, I'm lucky to have both luck in games and luck in love.

Why? In this context, "games" refers to gambling. For centuries, philosophers, including those from ancient Roman and Greek times, have associated gambling with negative connotations. Traditionally, someone who gambles was seen as having a troubled love life and a strained relationship with their partner, as they risked losing their belongings and family time. However, in modern German culture, the expression "unlucky in games, lucky in love" has taken on a more positive tone, serving as a way to comfort losers by reminding them that they may be winning in other areas of life.

1. Jemandem ist eine Laus über die Leber gelaufen
2. Das ist eine Ente
3. Ein Pechvogel sein
4. Ein Fischkopf sein
5. Einen Pferdefuß haben
6. Den Bock zum Gärtner machen
7. Mit jemandem Pferde stehlen können
8. Sich mit fremden Federn schmücken

– Hello.
– How is it going?
– What has run over his liver now?

Jemandem ist eine Laus über die Leber gelaufen

What? Literally: A louse has crawled over someone's liver.
Means: Being in a bad mood.

How? We've all been there before. Annoyed and in a terrible mood. That's when you use this expression. You're at work and your colleague isn't being his usual cheerful self, and his misery is sucking the energy out of the whole room. I mean, I won't judge him for that since I don't know what he's going through, but he probably has some lice running over his liver.

Why? In ancient and medieval medicine, the liver was associated with anger and negativity. And the louse in Germany has been used since the 16th century as an expression for something small and insignificant. By combining these two concepts, you get the idiom for someone being bothered or upset over something very minor. Even though the idea of lice over the liver sounds like a serious reason to visit the ER.

– Fake news
– The Pope will be the next president ...
– This is a duck!

What? Literally: That's a duck.
Means: That's fake news.

How? In the era of fake news and misinformation, we face daily challenges in distinguishing between real reports and completely fabricated ones. Is the Earth flat or round? Perhaps it's a cube, or better yet, a giant beer bottle. I saw that online and I'm not sure if it's true. Or was it just a duck, like a post from a hacker or bot?

Why? There's the expression "Zeitungsente", meaning "Newspaper Duck", which refers to fake, unsubstantiated claims often used in the news. The term might be a loanword from French, dating back to the 19th century, based on the expression "donner des canards", which means "to give ducks", a colloquialism for lying or spreading false information. Interestingly, there are also sources suggesting that the association of ducks with unreliability dates back to the 17th century or earlier, citing their unpredictable breeding habits as a reason for their perceived untrustworthiness. I love ducks so I refuse this claim.

– You are such a misfortune bird!

Ein Pechvogel sein

What? Literally: To be a misfortune bird.
Means: To be Unlucky.

How? An expression to describe an unlucky person. You trip on the sidewalk and fall, you're an unlucky bird. Or when you consistently attract mishaps and bad luck in general. I'm such an unlucky person. I always lose my keys, my glasses, and my phone. I'm such a *Pechvogel*.

Why? The idiom might be related to a medieval hunting practice where birds were caught using sticks smeared with lime, which were also called "Pechruten" or "lime rods". The birds would become stuck to the lime and unable to fly away, making them easy prey. This practice may have become a symbol for someone who has been dealt a bad hand by fate.

– Somewhere in Sylt …
– Why do you always go on holiday to the Fishheads?

Ein Fischkopf sein

What? Literally: To be a Fishhead.
Means: To be a north German.

How? Be cautious when using this term, as it can be a double-edged sword. On one hand, it's used as a colloquialism to affectionately refer to people from coastal regions in northern Germany, such as those near ports like Bremen and Hamburg. Your friend orders *Labskaus* instead of *Schnitzel* and you jokingly say, "Such a Fishhead!". On the other hand, it can be used in a derogatory manner, depending on the context. You might hear people describing themselves as such in the north, but I'd think twice before using it myself. Your "foreigner non-native not understanding the nuance of such expressions German card" might get revoked.

Why? I assume this one is self-explanatory. People in northern Germany live near the coast, where there's plenty of fish swimming around, or so I've heard. They eat a lot of seafood, *Fischbrötchen* fans to the front of the line.

– That has for sure a horse's foot.
– Buy now.
– Oh well!

Einen Pferdefuß haben

What? Literally: To have a horse's foot.
Means: There is something hidden.

How? Whenever something doesn't add up and you get suspicious that there's a catch. You get bombarded by ads every day in your inbox. And one of the ads catches your attention. It says "Buy our book and learn German in 3 days for free!" That sounds tempting, but there's something fishy and your spidey sense is tingling, so you click on the link and at the end it says delivery costs 50 euros. Ah ha!, that's where the *Pferdefuß* is! By the way, do check out our book *Jens and Jakob* to learn German. There are no hooves there, I promise!

Why? It may be attributed to an old folktale and superstition dating back to the 17th century, which associated horse's hooves with the devil. In Greek mythology, the god Pan was depicted with hooves, and similarly, the devil was often depicted with this attribute. This became a symbol for being seduced by an agreement or contract with hidden ulterior motives, much like the devil's own tactics.

– DEAL!
– I made the goat the gardener.

Den Bock zum Gärtner machen

What? Literally: To make the goat a gardener.
Means: To hire someone unsuitable.

How? Whenever someone unqualified is put in a position of decision-making or action, we say we made the goat a gardener. A typical example is when a politician gets elected despite having zero experience or background in the subject. Or, you ask your dear friend to watch over your children, who has no clue about kids, and when you come back home, the whole place is in a gigantic mess. In that case, you've made the goat a gardener!

Why? The idiom has written records dating back to the 16th century. A common theme in jewelry featured a goat munching on grass, which highlights the irony of expecting a goat to be a gardener, a contradictory notion. I would have thought that nobody knows more about plants than a goat, but it seems I was mistaken.

– My password is WhyDoGermansSayThat123.
– Do you trust him?
– Of course, with him you can steal horses.

Mit jemandem Pferde stehlen können

What? Literally: To be able to steal horses with someone.
Means: A reliable and trustworthy person.

How? To describe someone you can definitely rely on, you might hear something like, "Don't worry, you can trust me, I'm someone you can steal horses with!" This phrase can be used in personal friendships or transactional relationships, such as a boss telling his employees that they can share anything with him, because when it comes to horses and theft, he's your man!

Why? It may be as old as the 17th century in writing. Horses were considered a valuable commodity, and unsurprisingly, stealing horses was dealt a severe punishment. Therefore, the idea of trusting someone so much that you would steal a horse together, became a euphemism for a reliable and dependable character. I mean, that sounds quite sad for the horse, who didn't consent to being kidnapped.

– I pay a lot of attention to cleanliness.
– She always adorns herself with another's feathers!

Sich mit fremden Federn schmücken

What? Literally: To adorn oneself with another's feathers.
Means: To claim undeserved credit.

How? The expression is used whenever someone tries to take credit for someone else's achievement and work. When you work hard in a group project while the members sleep and play around, and then they claim the result as being of their own hard work, then they're trying to adorn themselves in someone else's feathers. I guess in this case, they adorned themselves with your feathers! Evil birds!

Why? The sad and depressing background of this idiom comes from a collection of fables by Phaedrus, which are a Latin adaptation of Aesop's Fables. The story has been reinterpreted in many cultures. The fable is about a crow who adorns itself with peacock feathers, but when it is exposed, the poor crow is mistreated, and its own feathers are eventually plucked out as a punishment. This fable is an old parable that warns people against pretending to be someone they're not. The story has many different variations.

1 Leben wie Gott in Frankreich
2 Gang nach Canossa
3 Einmal hü und einmal hott sagen
4 Schwedische Gardinen
5 Hinter dem Mond leben
6 Was für ein Tohuwabohu

– He only drinks good wine!
– ... and eats only good bread!
– He lives like God in France.

Leben wie Gott in Frankreich

What? Literally: To live like God in France.
Means: To live in luxury.

How? Ah, to live in luxury in France, even better to live like a deity in France. Enjoy a glass of wine, some good cheese (if you're not lactose intolerant), and munch on a croissant that you ordered from a local bakery, while the French judge your poor pronunciation through their raised eyebrows and squinted stare. It describes someone who enjoys life and lacks worry – a very lucky person.

Why? The idiom might be related to two possible sources, both of which convey the jealousy and impression that Germans have of the French living a life of opulence. One source predates the French Revolution, portraying the nobility and aristocracy as living like gods. The other one claims that after the revolution, the French lived in a state of freedom from God's commands and burdens, as if they had escaped the gaze of divine rule. Either way, enjoy your croissant.

– I didn't mean it that way.
– I'm sorry! I'm so sorry!
– This is a walk to Canossa.

Gang nach Canossa

What? Literally: Walk to Canossa.
Means: Groveling.

How? A poignant moment is when someone humbly asks for forgiveness, often a necessary step after causing harm. However, if someone demands an overly dramatic or exaggerated apology, implying a level of desperation, you might describe it as a "walk to Canossa," suggesting they're going to great lengths to make amends.

Why? The phrase comes from a notable event in the 11th century, when the Holy Roman Emperor Henry IV traveled to Canossa, Italy, to seek the Pope's pardon for his actions, which were seen as an overreach of his authority, and to avoid being put to death. He spent days on his knees at the gate's entrance, begging for mercy. If you're wondering whether his groveling spared his life, it did. Today, this is used to describe an act of excessive groveling or begging for forgiveness, often in a humiliating or over-the-top manner.

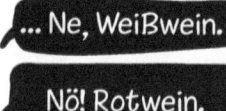

– Red wine.
– Prefer beer! ... No, white wine. Nope! Red wine. ... Apple spritzer. Or rosé wine!
– I would have preferred to order beer.
– To say sometimes *hü*, and sometimes *hott*.

Einmal hü und einmal hott sagen

What? Literally: To say sometimes left, and sometimes right.
Means: Constantly changing your mind.

How? To describe someone who is notoriously indecisive and can't seem to make up their mind, and even the simplest decisions become a long and arduous process. If you're planning a weekend party with friends like this, you might avoid asking for their input, knowing it could take weeks for them to decide. Instead, you might just take the reins and suggest the restaurant yourself, saving yourself the frustration of their indecisiveness. Sometimes *hü*, sometimes *hott*!

Why? This comes from carriage drivers and how they commanded the animals to follow directions. Telling the horse to turn *hü* left, or *hott* right. This turned into an idiomatic expression for not taking sides or sticking to one opinion.

– Behind Swedish curtains, you criminal.

Schwedische Gardinen

What? Literally: Swedish curtains.
Means: Prison.

How? This has a direct simple meaning, to sit behind bars! You should be careful of *Schwarzfahren* in Germany, otherwise you might end up behind Swedish curtains. I am sure a Swedish person might get very confused when they hear this expression. Even more funny to think about, a Swedish person is sitting behind Swedish curtains. For me it sounds like a product from IKEA.

Why? The idiom actually has a connection to Sweden, and more specifically to Swedish steel, which was renowned for its high quality and used to produce prison bars. The expression dates back to the 1900s. I wonder if IKEA produces prison bars. They do have baby cribs that, in a humorous way, resemble tiny prisons.

- You don't know what Skapago is?
- You surely live behind the moon!

Hinter dem Mond leben

What? Literally: To live behind the moon.
Means: To be uninformed and backwards.

How? It describes a person who is disconnected from the world and unaware of what's happening around them. In English, we'd say someone who is "living under a rock." You have a conversation with your friend and they seem completely oblivious to current events, like inflation, and you're shocked, thinking, "Do you live behind the moon?" It also implies someone who is not modern and hasn't kept up with the times. For example, if your friend sends you a letter, you might say, "Are you living behind the moon? Just text me instead!"

Why? We all know that the moon has a side we can't see, since it orbits the Earth, facing away from our view. If you're not aware of this basic fact, you might be considered to live behind the moon! The expression has become synonymous with someone who is completely unaware, as if they live on the hidden side of the moon, cut off from the rest of the world. You might also hear *auf dem Mond leben*, to live on the moon.

– Such a mess!

Was für ein Tohuwabohu

What? Literally: A desolate and empty land.
Means: A mess, chaos.

How? I love this expression. Imagine the ultimate fear of any stereotypical German: a chaotic mess! Whenever you see something disorganized and untidy, you'd say "Tohuwabohu." A classic scenario would be leaving the kids you're babysitting to play in their room while you go make some tea, only to return and find the place turned into a whirlwind of chaos. It's a miracle they managed to turn their environment upside down in such a short time. What a *Tohuwabohu*! Take a sip of your chamomile tea and try to relax.

Why? The idiom "tōhū wā-bōhū" originates from Hebrew and is found in the Old Testament. Its original meaning is a desolate and empty land. However, over time, the connotation of the word has shifted, and today it's used to describe a complete and utter chaos, a disordered mess without structure or rules.

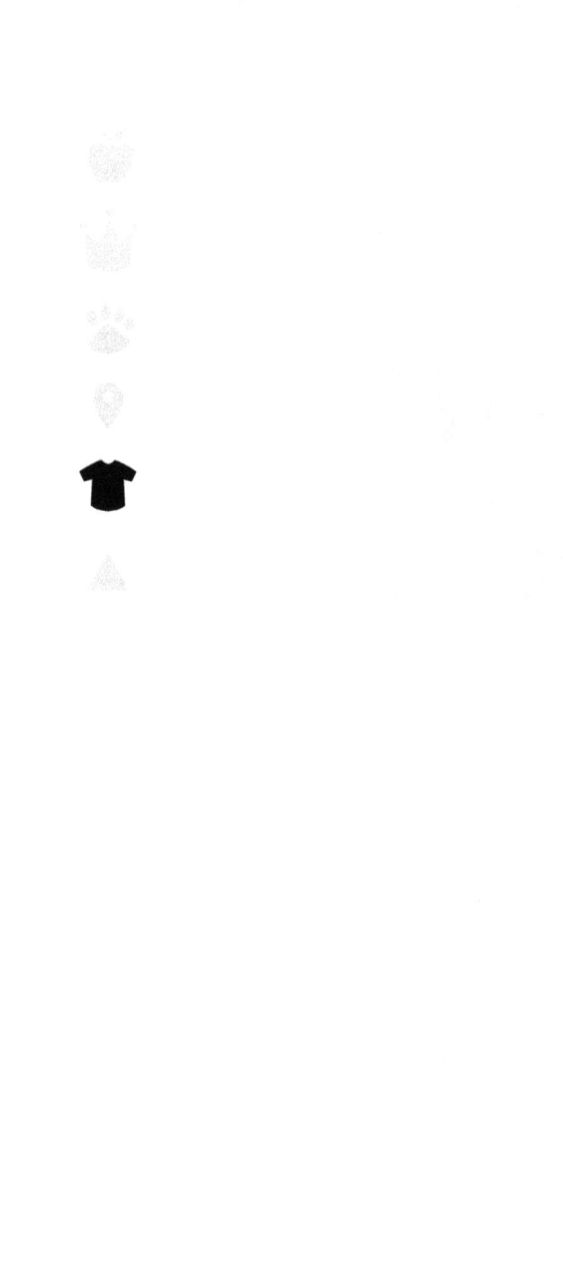

CLOTHES & BODY

1. Das letzte Hemd hat keine Taschen
2. Alte Zöpfe abschneiden
3. Hals- und Beinbruch!
4. Jacke wie Hose
5. Das passt wie die Faust aufs Auge
6. Haare auf den Zähnen haben
7. Das Handtuch werfen

– Donation
– The last shirt has no pockets.

Das letzte Hemd hat keine Taschen

What? Literally: The last shirt has no pockets.
Means: In death, one cannot take any earthly goods.

How? It usually implies that there is no point in holding on to materialistic possessions for tomorrow when one can share or use them today. For example, you want to book a fancy restaurant for Valentine's Day and the prices are making you second-guess, but then you think to yourself, "Ah, whatever, the last shirt has no pockets; let's enjoy a little." Or in the context of donation, when you receive a spam email that says an old billionaire on his deathbed wants to give you all his money because he can't take it to his grave. What's the point of keeping it? In case that happens to you and it isn't spam, please wire me a commission. Your last shirt doesn't have pockets.

Why? It might have roots in the old traditional practice in funerals, where the deceased was dressed in simple white garments called a *Totenhemd* or *Sterbehemd*, meaning "deceased shirt," which had no pockets stitched in them. Hence the idiom. It's actually a comforting thought when you lose materialistic possessions. It's okay, we can't take them to the grave, our shirts have no pockets.

– Year 1900
– Pants are for men!
– Time to cut off the old braids.

Alte Zöpfe abschneiden

What? Literally: To cut off old braids.
Means: Abandon old habits.

How? A very common idiom that refers to giving up on old, useless traditions or habits. You might hear it in a political context, like, "It's time for a reform and to cut loose old braids." Or in a personal situation, like, "I should sell my Telefax, I barely use it. It's time to cut off old braids."

Why? Braids and wigs were a common hairstyle for men, especially among the nobility and soldiers in the 18th century. Even commoners would try to imitate them. However, the French Revolution changed the perspective on them, associating them with backwardness and ridicule. Cutting them off became a symbol of modernity. This was seen at the Wartburg Festival in 1817, where 500 people gathered to protest for a united Germany and freedom for the people: The symbolic cutting and burning of their old braids marked a desire for a new era and a departure from outdated institutions and ideas. They also burned the books of their rivals, marking a significant moment in German history.

– Oh, you're going to the mountains with
the donkeys? Broken neck and leg!

Hals- und Beinbruch!

What? Literally: Broken neck and leg.
Means: Good luck.

How? It is similar to the English saying "Break a leg!" When your friend is going to an exam and you want to wish him good luck, you'd say in German "Broken neck and leg!" (all the best). Or if your friend is worried about his mountain trip, you can reassure him by saying "Don't worry, you can do it, broken neck and leg!"

Why? This phrase might originate from a misunderstanding of the Yiddish saying "hazlacha ve-bracha", which means "good luck and blessings". Due to the language barrier, the Germans may have misinterpreted it as "Hals- und Beinbruch". Another possible origin is the old folk superstition that one can ward off evil by wishing for the opposite, such as wishing someone an injury. In this context, when men went on a hunt, people would wish them a broken bone.

– We're late ... Just take any tie. It's jackets like pants.

Jacke wie Hose

What? Literally: Jackets like pants.
Means: The same thing.

How? You'd say this either in a non-figurative sense, like not caring about your wardrobe or which piece of clothing fits with which, or when deciding which restaurant to go to on the weekend, Italian or German, and you'd say, "Either one – jackets like pants." Or in a metaphorical way, like saying that you don't see any importance in differentiating between "Sie" and "Du".

Why? The idiom actually has a literal meaning and a historical context, with written records dating back to the 17th century. In the past, jackets and pants were not made from the same material. Eventually, it became a common practice to use the same fabric for both. Tailors would advertise their new trend by saying that they were selling "Jackets like Pants", which eventually became a metaphor for anything being equivalent or interchangeable.

– I look great with these glasses and my outfit.
– This fits like the fist on the eye.

Das passt wie die Faust aufs Auge

What? Literally: That fits like the fist on the eye.
Means: Doesn't fit together, or fits together.

How? This is a confusing one with a generational gap. It can both mean fitting together or not fitting together, depending on the context and probably the generation of the person using it. You might use this idiom when someone suggests eating schnitzel and sushi together, and your head spins, thinking "those two don't go together, like a fist on the eye." Alternatively, you might hear the opposite form from a boss who says, "You're amazing and our company is amazing. We fit together like a fist on the eye." In this case, it implies a great match or harmony. A double-edged sword, as he might have meant it negatively too.

Why? Its use has been popular since the Middle Ages. In a literal sense, a fist on the eye would be an unfortunate mix, one that you'd want to avoid, unless you enjoy pain. However, over time, the meaning shifted to a more ironic use, where things actually do fit together. It's interesting to see how contradictory meanings can evolve, like a fist on the eye.

– We forgot about our homework ...
– Oh dear, that's going to cause trouble.
The teacher has hair on the teeth.

Haare auf den Zähnen haben

What? Literally: To have hair on the teeth.
Means: Someone difficult to get along with, argumentative.

How? It generally has a negative and derogatory connotation, describing someone who is opinionated and rarely compromises. For example, your boss who is overly critical and will yell at you when you don't finish a project on time, "has hair on his teeth". It can also be a positive attribute, meaning someone who doesn't back off and will take action. When your friend recommends a lawyer to represent you who will defend you in court and takes no nonsense from anybody, then he also has hair on the teeth.

Why? It relates to an outdated view that hairiness was a masculine characteristic, symbolizing strength and confidence, to the point where someone is even described as having hair on their teeth. This person is someone who doesn't take no for an answer and is consequently difficult to get along with. Originally, this term was a negative and insulting label for women, but its meaning has since expanded to apply to anyone.

– And Go! ... 1! 2!
– 3! Now you've thrown the towel?

Das Handtuch werfen

What? Literally: To throw the towel.
Means: To give up.

How? We have the same expression in English, to throw in the towel. It means someone completely quits. You got excited at the beginning of the year to start your New Year's resolution of joining the gym and working on your physique, but after a couple of weeks you realize life is more fun being lazy, so you decide to throw in the towel. You keep sending emails to your internet provider to update your information that you got married and changed your name, but they never respond, so you throw in the towel.

Why? Not sure if you're into boxing, but that's where the idiom originates. In boxing, when a fighter is losing and there's no sign of hope to win, the trainer would throw in the towel to signal to the referee that they're conceding the match and accepting defeat.

▲

1 Im Eimer sein
2 Auf dem Holzweg sein
3 Jemanden über den grünen Klee loben
4 In die Röhre gucken
5 Auf dem Schlauch stehen
6 Es ist höchste Eisenbahn
7 Buch mit sieben Siegeln
8 Etwas auf dem Schirm haben
9 Durch den Wind sein
10 In ein Loch fallen

– Because of Corona the beach is closed.
– Oh no, our weekend is in the bucket.

Im Eimer sein

What? Literally: To be in the bucket.
Means: Something is ruined.

How? This expression has different meanings. It might refer to something that's physically damaged, like saying my mobile fell and now it's broken. It's in the bucket. Or it might mean being completely exhausted, like I was jogging for hours and now I'm completely in the bucket and need to rest. And of course, plans being derailed, like canceling a trip because of the weather.

Why? This idiom has a literal meaning of being in the trash, as in being in the *Abfalleimer*, meaning the garbage can. Something is damaged and destined for disposal, whether literally or figuratively speaking.

– This is how I will reach B1 without studying.
– He's surely on the woodpath!

Auf dem Holzweg sein

What? Literally: To be on the woodpath.
Means: To be wrong.

How? We'd use this expression when someone is using the wrong method in order to reach their goal. You might hear someone commenting that if the political party thinks that reforming this law will solve the problem then they're completely on the wrong track, or in German, on the woodpath.

Why? The idiom has been documented since the Middle Ages and originated with lumberjacks. A *Holzweg* refers to the path leading into the forest where they harvested wood. Many hikers would mistakenly follow this path, only to reach a dead end and have to return. Hence the idiom, being on the woodpath.

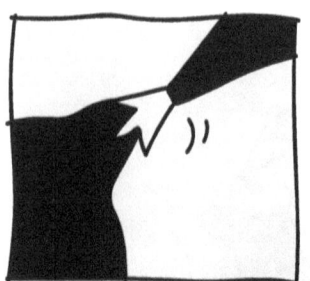

– A GENIUS! AWESOME. A REAL GENIUS!
– So pretty too! Marry me, you genius!!!
– They're praising him over the green clover.

Jemanden über den grünen Klee loben

What? Literally: To praise someone over the green clover.
Means: To overly praise someone.

How? Whether deserved or not, this means over-the-top compliments and praise for someone. When you're watching an award show and they applaud for hours for the artist of the year who strung two chords together to create their masterpiece song, "I'm Better Than You," you might say they were praised over the green clover. A similar idiom in English is "praised to the skies" or "praised to the heavens."

Why? The origin of the expression is unclear, but in medieval poetry, clover was often associated with lovers and spring, and was frequently used in writings to describe them. Another possible source dates back to the traditional practice of planting clover on graves, where it was considered impolite to speak ill of the dead. In either case, clover became a symbol of compliments and love, which may have led to the phrase. In a way, it could mean to praise someone more lavishly than poets praise clover.

– For sale.
– I looked in the tube.
– Sold

In die Röhre gucken

What? Literally: Looking into the tube.
Means: To get nothing.

How? Whenever you miss the chance to get something and come out empty-handed. You kept thinking about booking the hotel room or not, wondering if the location is good and if the price is worth it, and at the end someone booked it and you wasted your time. Or when you're not even included in benefiting from something, you're simply a bystander. All metro users will get a discount, but unfortunately for all the bus takers, they're left looking into the tube.

Why? It's plausible that the meaning is quite literal, and comes from hunting. Hunters refer to animal dens, such as those of rabbits, foxes, or badgers, as *Röhren*. When the animal flees back into its den, the hunters are left looking into the tube, and they're forced to come back empty-handed.

– Germany or Ger-few?
– He's clearly standing on the hose.

Auf dem Schlauch stehen

What? Literally: To stand on the hose.
Means: To not comprehend.

How? There are multiple possible uses for this expression. One common one is feeling confused or not understanding something. For example, when struggling with your project and asking your colleague for help, you might say, "I'm standing on the hose. I need your advice." Another meaning is being held back or unable to progress. For instance, waiting for a confirmation from your boss about your vacation request, you might tell your friend, "If my boss doesn't reply this week, I won't be able to book the flight and I'll be standing on the hose." A less common meaning is being in trouble. For example, if you lose your phone, you might say, "If I lose my phone, I won't be able to use my bank apps and I'll be standing on the hose."

Why? There are multiple theories on its origin. They all share a similar connotation, which is that standing on the hose will obstruct the flow and hinder it. One possible background of the idiom comes from firemen, who would cut off the water flow if one stood on the hose. However, I'm not convinced that the pressure of the water wouldn't be stronger than a firefighter's weight, though they are muscular and strong so I might be wrong.

– Your train is leaving soon ... right?!
– It is the highest train.

Es ist höchste Eisenbahn

What? Literally: It is the highest train.
Means: It is very urgent.

How? You're in a crunch for time, and you have to start something now, otherwise it will be too late. Your boss might email you that the project deadline is nearing, and it's *höchste Eisenbahn* to work on it urgently. Or your guests are visiting in an hour, and your apartment is a complete mess. You want to clean up as soon as possible before they arrive, it's *höchste Eisenbahn* to begin.

Why? The expression originates from a comedy by the Berlin humorist Adolf Glaßbrenner in the 19th century. The protagonist of the play is a postman who confuses words. In the midst of a conversation, he wants to excuse himself to leave because the train has arrived and he needs to collect the letters. He intends to say "Es ist höchste Zeit, die Eisenbahn ist schon angekommen," which means "It is high time, the train has arrived." However, he gets it wrong and says "Es ist höchste Eisenbahn, die Zeit ist schon angekommen," which is absurdly translated to "It is high train, the time has arrived." This phrase has become a popular idiom to this day.

– The yogurt tastes good!
– (masculine or feminine) ... the yogurt?
– German grammar is a book with seven seals!

...des Joghurtes?!

Buch mit sieben Siegeln

What? Literally: Book with seven seals.
Means: Something incomprehensible.

How? Use this to describe something or someone who is difficult to decipher and understand. When older people think that kids these days are so complicated, they might say that kids these days are a book with seven seals. Or, the manual of how to assemble a table says on the top, printed in bold, "Our instructions are simple, not a book with seven seals."

Why? The number 7 has many connotations of being a sacred and magical number. In many ancient civilizations, such as Greece, Babylon, Sumeria, and Rome, the number 7 held a significant meaning. This is also reflected in the Old Testament, where God created existence in 7 days, and there are 7 archangels, among other references. The idiom originates from the Book of Revelation: "And I saw in the right hand of him who sat on the throne a book written inside and out, sealed with seven seals. And I saw a strong angel calling with a loud voice: Who is worthy to open the book and break its seals? And no one, neither in heaven nor on earth nor under the earth, was able to open the book and look into it." This passage has become the basis for the idiom, which describes something that is almost impossible to understand or decipher.

– Do you still have the gifts on your screen? Tomorrow is Christmas!

Etwas auf dem Schirm haben

What? Literally: Have something on your screen.
Means: To not forget something.

How? Similar to the English idiom "on the radar," this expression can be used to describe having something in your mind that you shouldn't forget, such as a future plan. For example, you might be trying to remember to buy a gift for a friend's birthday. Alternatively, it can also be used to describe something that you're not aware of, such as when you're asking a friend about possible plans for the weekend and you ask them, "Are there any more suggestions I forgot that aren't on my radar?"

Why? It originated from the radar screens used to locate and detect aircraft flying around. It's not as old as some of the other idioms in the book, being a relatively recent expression, dating back to the late 20th century. For a long time, I thought the phrase meant "auf dem Regenschirm," meaning "under the umbrella," but I still prefer the incorrect visual association I made as an alternative.

– How has he been doing since he was fired?
– He is through the wind!

Durch den Wind sein

What? Literally: To be through the wind.
Means: In a bad shape.

How? Try to imagine this expression visually: someone struggling through the wind as it blows him ferociously, pushing him back and forth. That's what the idiom means in a figurative way. When your thoughts are unclear and you're exhausted and distracted, you're "through the wind."

Why? This phrase comes from sailors. When a storm blows, the ship is tossed about, making it difficult for the sailors to keep their bearings and steer in the right direction. The turmoil of the situation leaves the sailors fatigued and exhausted, which is where the colloquial expression comes from.

– She's fallen into a hole since I switched from wet to dry food.

In ein Loch fallen

What? Literally: To fall into a hole.
Means: To become depressed.

How? I'm happy to end this with a depressing idiom, because it is sad that you reached the end of the book, and I hope you get to enjoy your journey exploring German. In case you are miserable and beyond sad then that's a perfect situation to use this expression. You fell in a hole!

Why? Unfortunately, this phrase has no known origin other than the figurative description of its meaning. To fall into a hole is neither enjoyable nor a desirable experience. I assume that's where it comes from, as with similar phrases like "In ein schwarzes Loch fallen" or "In ein tiefes Loch fallen" which are equivalent to "falling into a black hole" or "falling into a deep hole," which are unpleasant experiences one hopes to avoid. May you never fall in one.

SKAPAGO

Online language learning and textbooks.

Herzlichen Glückwunsch!

You've made it to the end of the book!
Now, it's time to show off your knowledge of German idioms.
But wait, there's more!

If you're hooked on learning German, I've got just the thing for you. I learned German with the help of "Jens und Jakob", a fantastic book that's also available as an online course. It's a story-based approach that breaks down the language in a way that's easy to understand. And the best part? We now have books available for both beginners and intermediate learners, at A level and B level.

And if you're feeling adventurous, you can explore other languages with Skapago's range of courses.

Happy Learning!

Tschüss!
Bis nächstes Mal.

Max . Skalla

www.ingramcontent.com/pod-product-compliance
Lightning Source LLC
LaVergne TN
LVHW092008090526
838202LV00002B/51